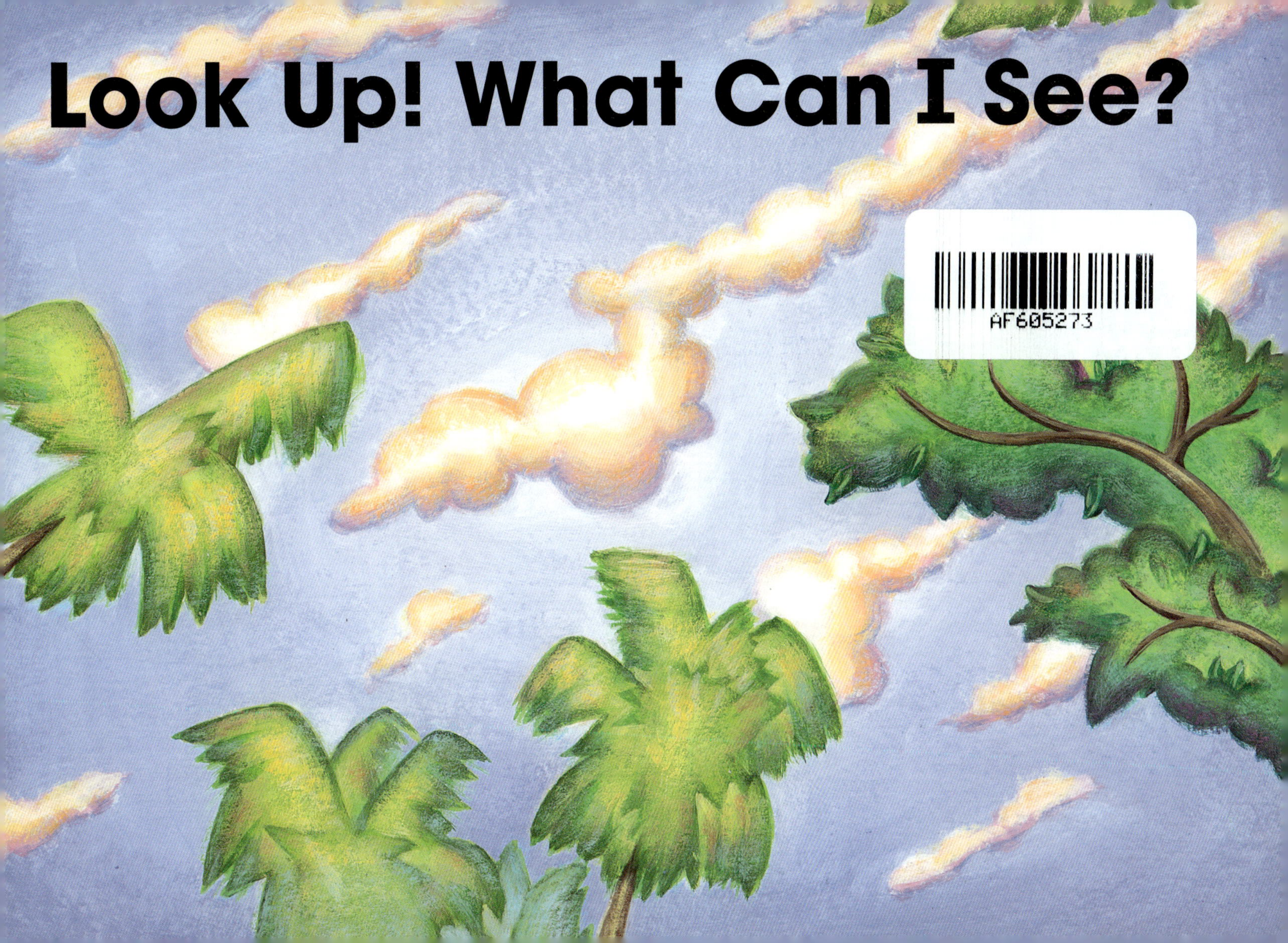
Look Up! What Can I See?

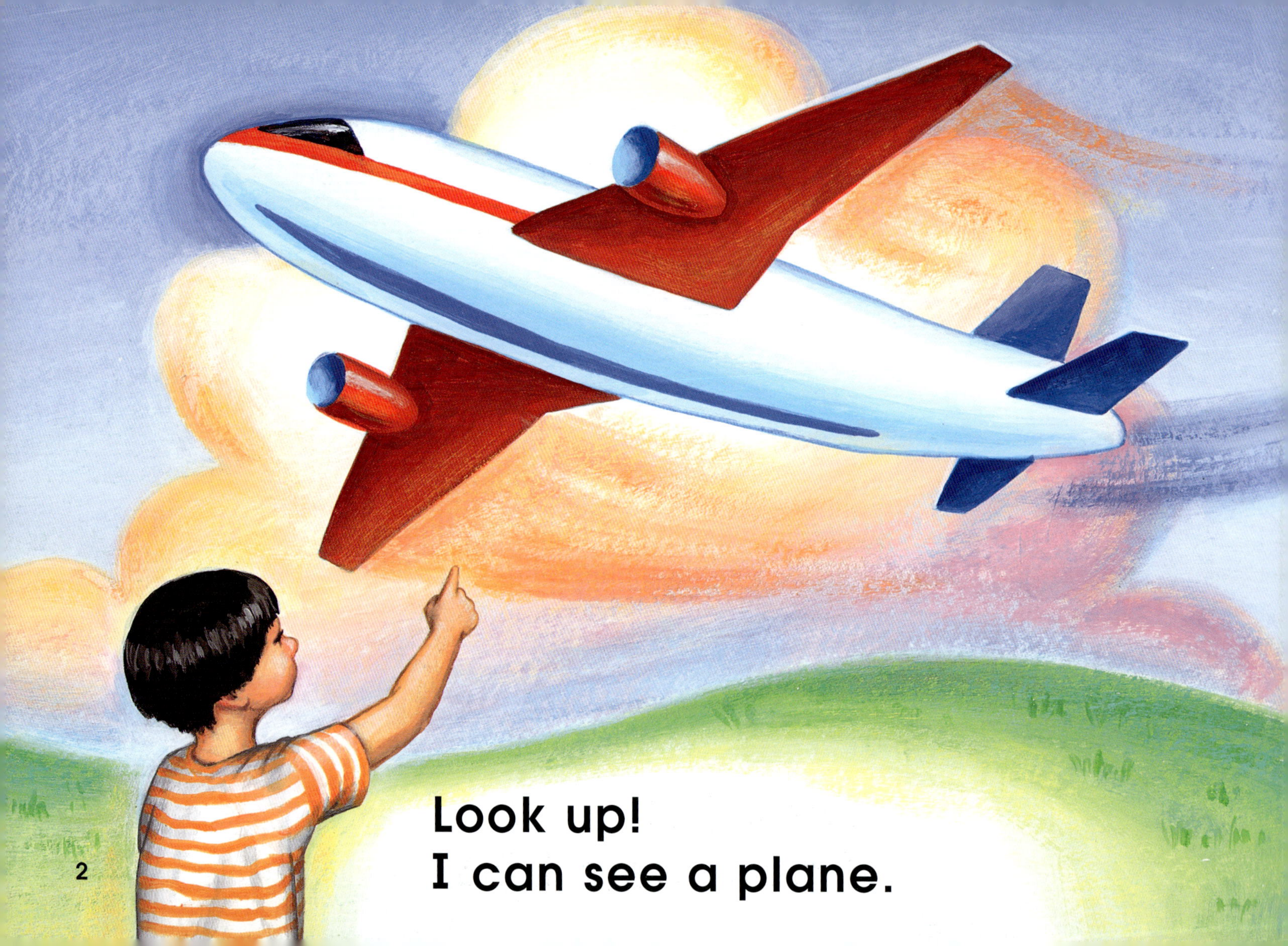

Look up!
I can see a plane.

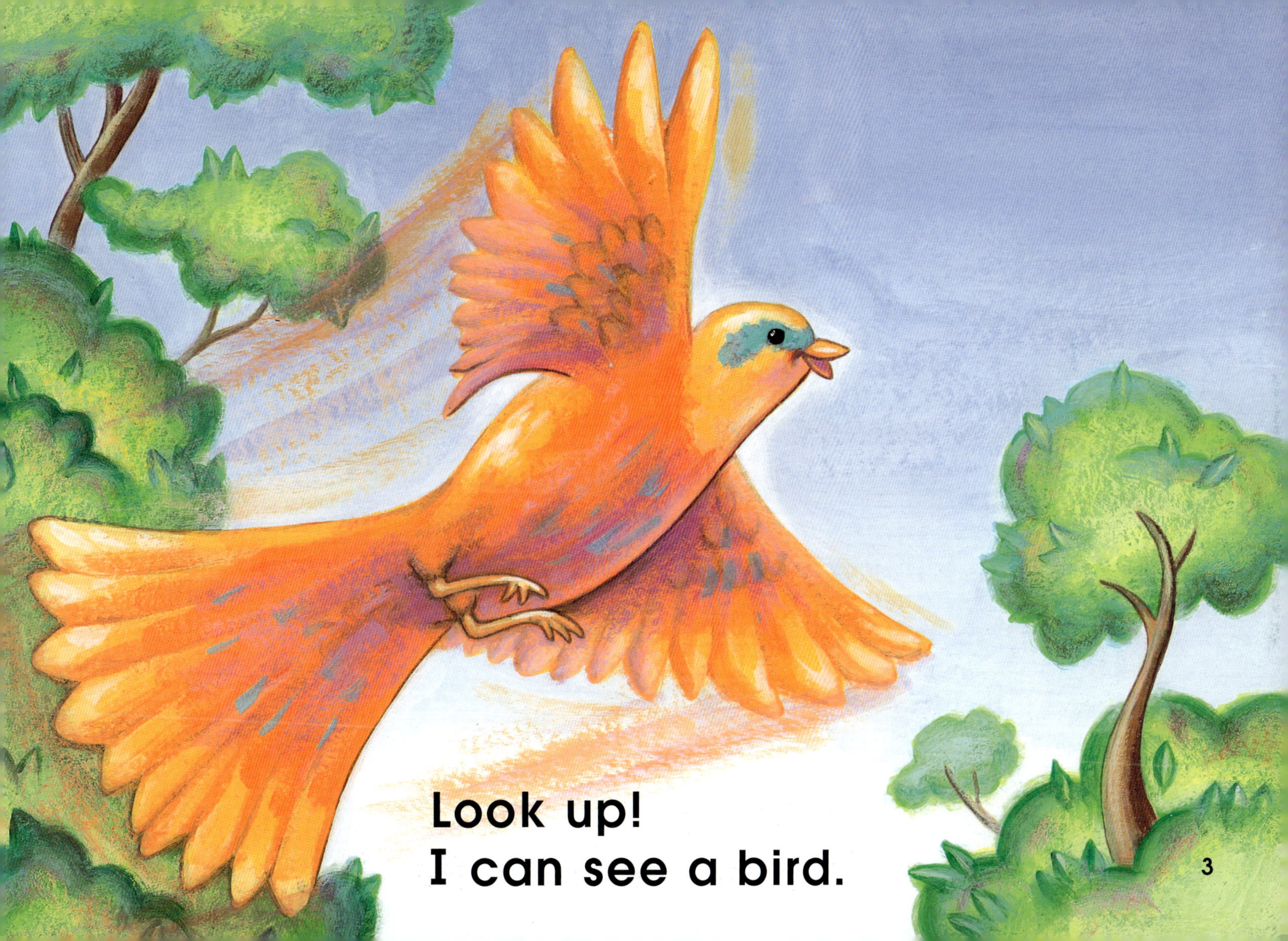

Look up!
I can see a bird.

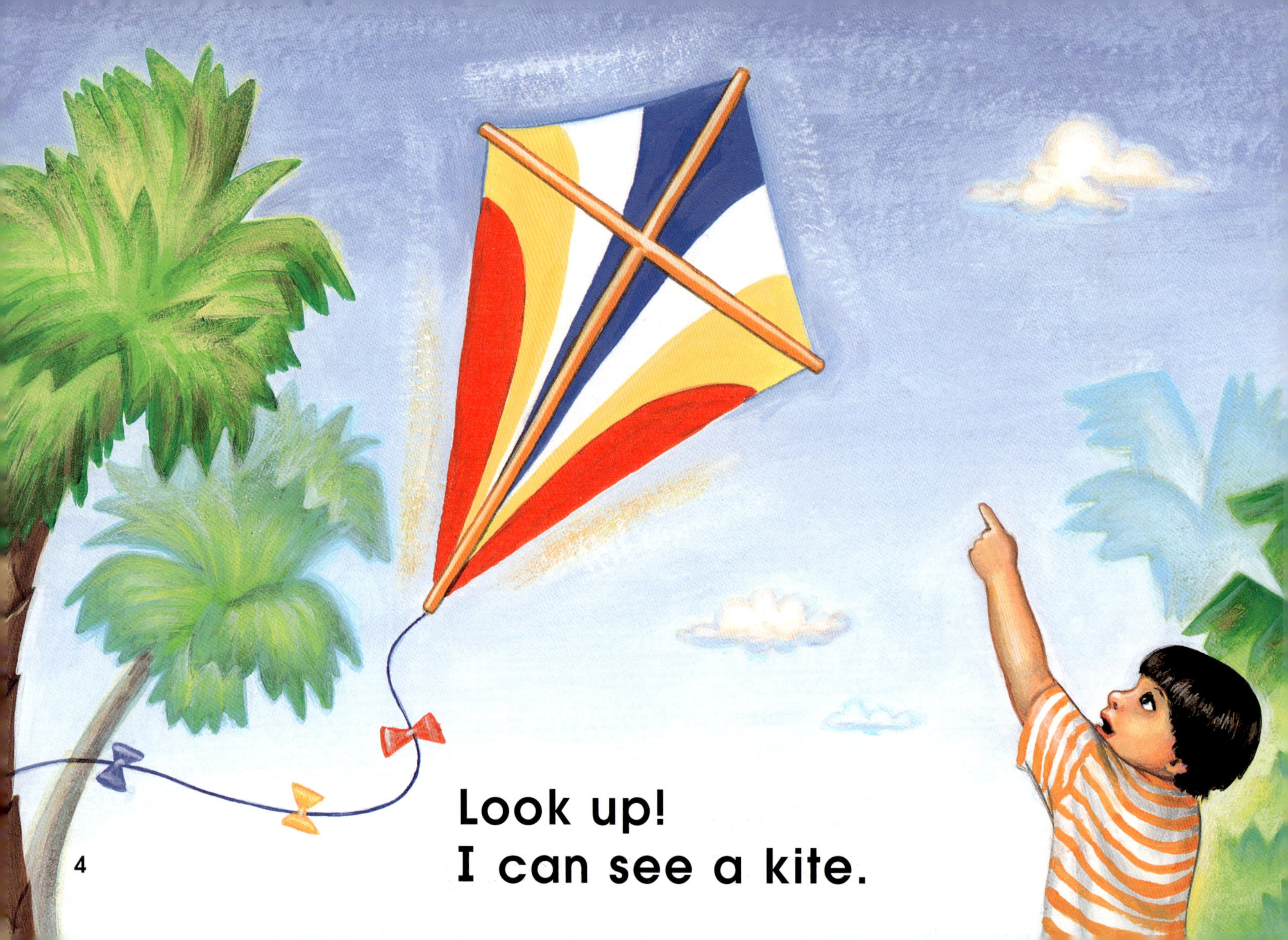

Look up!
I can see a kite.

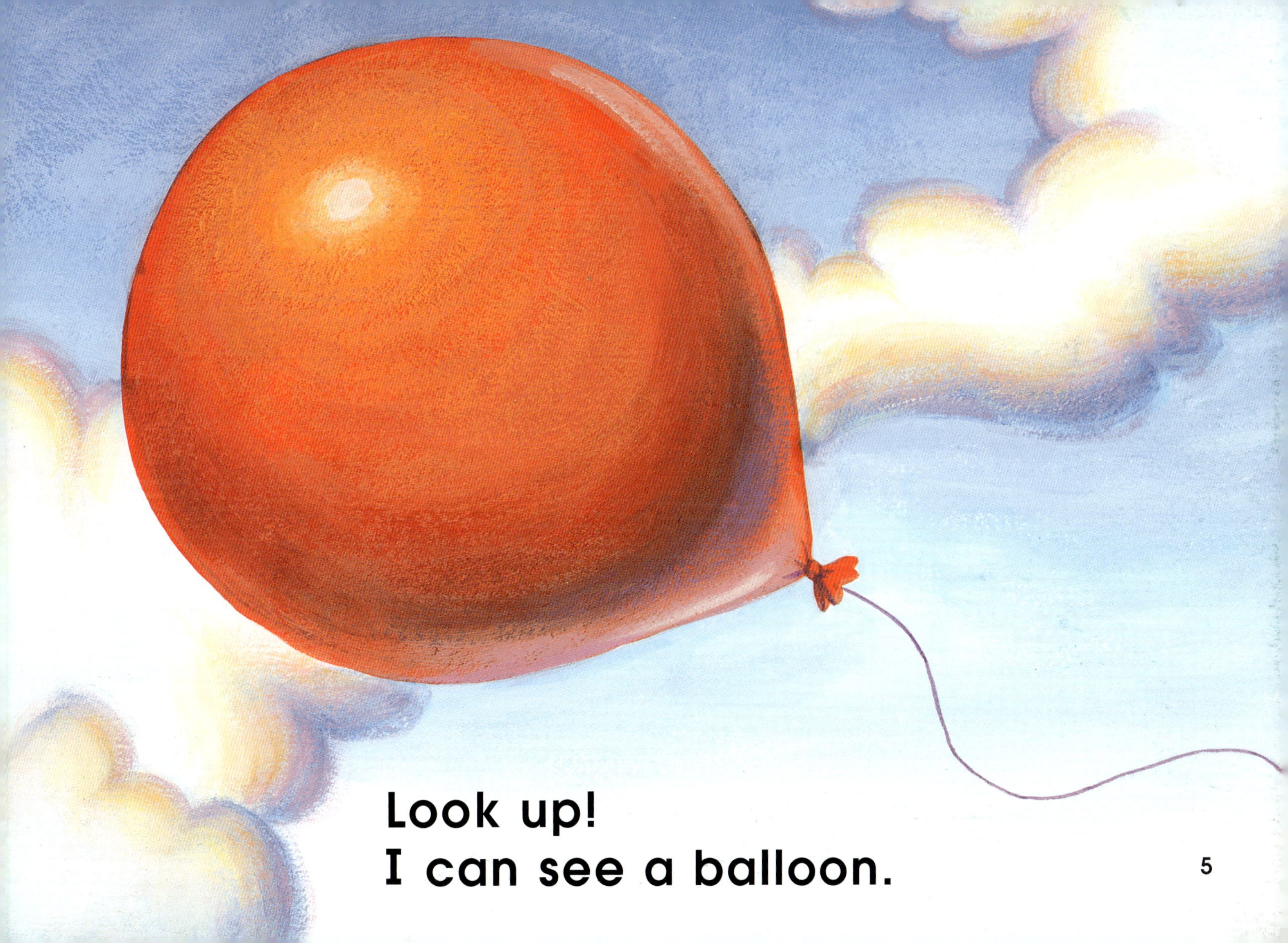
Look up!
I can see a balloon.

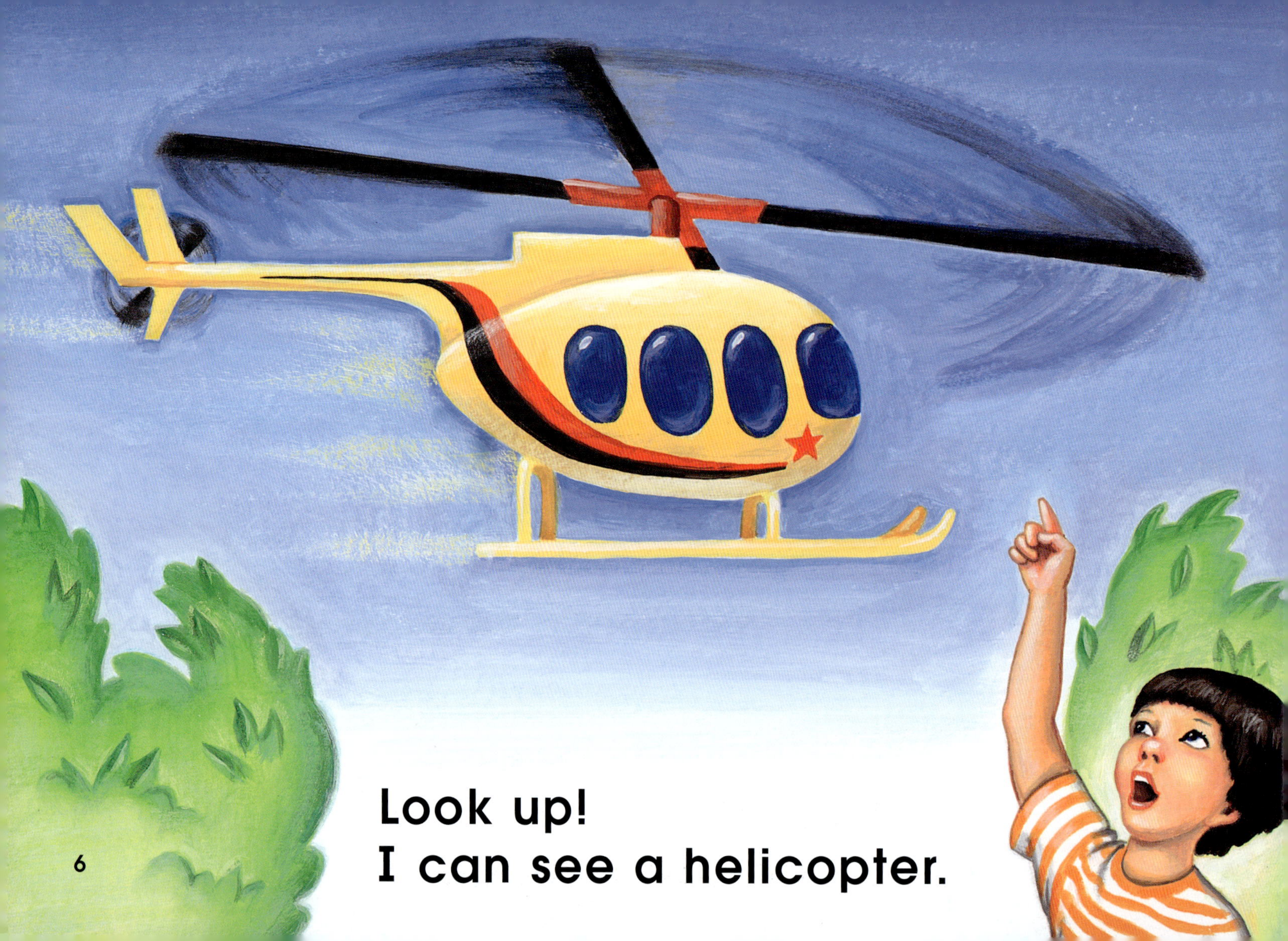

Look up!
I can see a helicopter.

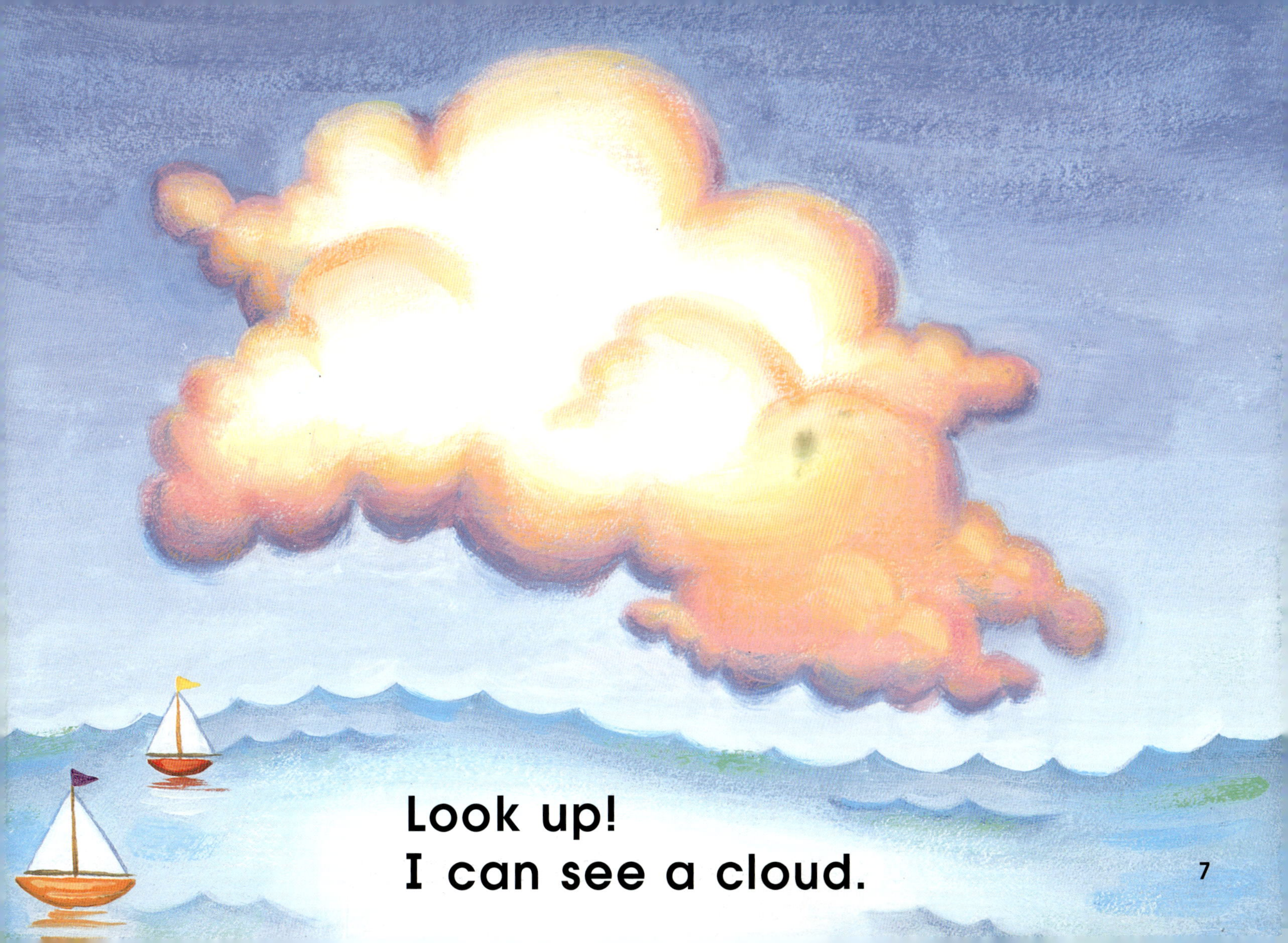

Look up!
I can see a cloud.

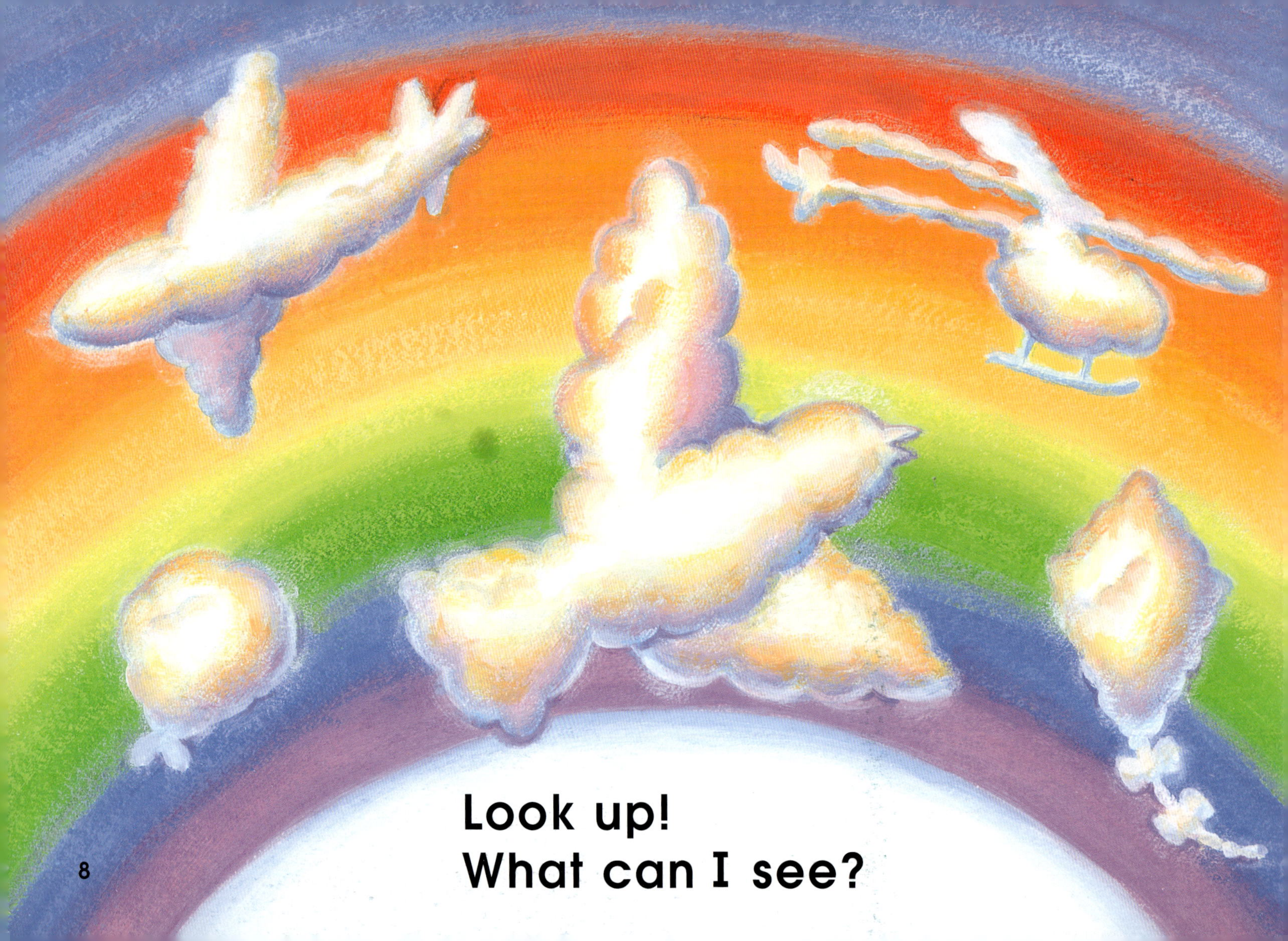

Look up!
What can I see?